3 180078 581

**Report by the
Comptroller and Auditor General**

GW00372493

Managing the
Millennium Threat

Ordered by the
House of Commons
to be printed 15 May 1997

LONDON: The Stationery Office

£4.70

HC 3 Session 1997–98

Published 21 May 1997

This report has been prepared under Section 6 of the National Audit Act 1983 for presentation to the House of Commons in accordance with Section 9 of the Act.

John Bourn
Comptroller and Auditor General

National Audit Office
7 May 1997

The Comptroller and Auditor General is the head of the National Audit Office employing some 750 staff. He, and the National Audit Office, are totally independent of Government. He certifies the accounts of all Government departments and a wide range of other public sector bodies; and he has statutory authority to report to Parliament on the economy, efficiency and effectiveness with which departments and other bodies have used their resources.

Contents

Part 1: The Millennium Threat

Summary

1.1 In the last two decades of the 20th Century, much of government business and daily life has come to rely on information systems. If many of these information systems are not modified they will not be able to continue functioning correctly in the year 2000. This could mean salaries not paid, invoices not being issued, collection of taxes put at risk, defence systems malfunctioning, inaccurate hospital records, interest on savings not paid and mortgage payments suddenly increased. It could even mean security locks failing to open and air conditioning systems shutting down and credit cards expiring on 31st December 1999. The government's Central Computer and Telecommunications Agency has described it as the biggest crisis the information technology industry has ever faced. The impact on organisations that use information technology could be calamitous.

1.2 This report describes the problem, why it has happened and what is being done centrally by government to ensure routine government business can continue in the year 2000. For departments and agencies the key findings are that:

- most are aware of the problem;

- most are at the stage of auditing their systems;

- four-fifths of them were confident that they will complete the work in time;

- at this stage it is not possible to estimate costs with confidence.

1.3 We plan to publish a further report updating progress and describing in more detail how some departments are tackling the problem.

The problem

1.4 Many information systems only use two numbers to represent the year, so that, for example, 1999 will be stored by the computer as '99'. The year 2000 will be represented by '00', and these information systems will assume that 00 comes before 99. This will affect any computer application which involves calculations based

1

on dates. For example, a program run in the year 2000 to calculate the age of someone born in 1930 for pension purposes would take the current year (00) less the year of birth (30) and could end up with an age of 30.

1.5 The way information systems might react on 1st January 2000 varies considerably. Some systems may not be able to cope and will simply shut down. Others may continue to function but produce meaningless results if they assume that 00 comes before 99. Others may revert to whatever the date was when the systems were first programmed or to some other base date such as 1980.

1.6 This is an international problem and does not only affect computer programs. Control systems in other equipment, such as lifts, air conditioning systems, security systems and even home video systems and traffic lights often use computer chips which control dates. All of these could be affected.

1.7 A further problem is that the year 2000 is a leap year, but some systems incorrectly assume it is not. Any application on these computers will assume the 29th February 2000 does not exist.

The consequences

1.8 Any computer application which uses dates could be affected if no action is taken. This could mean:

- Hospital records and patient information being dangerously inaccurate through computers calculating patients' ages to be negative;

- Police records being lost;

- If companies' payroll and accounting systems fail, the free flow of income tax and VAT to the Exchequer being put at risk;

- Defence systems malfunctioning, including weapon and command and control systems;

- Mortgages and investments failing as computers miscalculate interest, terminate such arrangements early or add 100 years to the terms of others;

- Salaries not being paid;

- Savings and loans attracting 100 years interest overnight.

1.9 Difficulties have already arisen where information systems are used to plan ahead. A large food retailer uses a computer to monitor sell by dates. The computer interpreted '00' as representing 1900 and issued instructions for a large quantity of food to be destroyed as it assumed the food was well past its sell by date. A survey by PA Consulting Group and Taskforce 2000 carried out in November 1996 found that 86 per cent of those organisations affected by the problem believed they would be impacted before the year 2000, including 19 per cent who say they have already been affected.

The reasons

1.10 In the 1960s and 1970s it was very common to use two numbers to represent the year. This saved valuable memory for processing data and disc space for storing it. Programmers at that time did not expect the systems to remain in use for more than 10 years. Many older systems or components are still running 30 years later.

1.11 Most newer systems have been designed to cope with the millennium, but some still use two digits to represent the year, partly from inertia but also to maintain compatibility with earlier systems.

1.12 The leap year problem has been caused by incomplete knowledge of the rules governing leap years. A year which is a multiple of 100 such as 1900 is not a leap year unless it is also a multiple of 400, such as 2000.

The solutions

1.13 Firstly there is a need for managers at all levels to be aware that this is not just a technical issue, but one which can have a profound impact on the ability of the organisation to continue functioning in the next millennium. Although in most cases it is fairly simple to modify the way an information system stores dates, the number of modifications needed in most organisations makes this a huge programme to manage.

1.14 Box 1 shows the key stages of an action plan to ensure all information systems can cope with the millennium.

Box 1: Key stages

Assign clear responsibility for year 2000 compliance

Create an inventory of systems

Audit all systems for compliance by January 1997

Produce a prioritised list of systems requiring modification

Estimate costs

Finalise a prioritised, costed, timed programme of action by October 1997

Manage the programme to budget and time

Test all modified systems by January 1999

1.15 A serious constraint is the shortage of suitably skilled staff in the community at large to manage the programme and make the modifications. There are already indications that the cost of employing these staff is rising as demand for their skills increases.

The costs

1.16 At this stage estimates are very vague as many companies and government departments have not completed the audit of their systems, nor in some cases established who has legal liability for the modifications.

1.17 It has been suggested that many of the companies in the FT250 list and some government departments could face costs of between £10-£60 million each. The PA Consulting Group/Taskforce 2000 survey found that 69 per cent of organisations believe it will cost them more than £500,000 to fix the problems with 10 per cent of them expecting a bill in excess of £10 million.

1.18 For comparison, the US House of Representatives estimated in July 1996 that the cost of modifying Federal systems could be as much as $30 billion.

Part 2: Central Government's response

Responsibility for action

2.1 The responsibility for ensuring that information systems in the public sector can handle dates correctly in the year 2000 lies with individual departments and agencies. Centrally, the Cabinet Office through the Office of Public Service have made all departments aware of the problem and set targets for key stages of departmental action plans.

2.2 Within the Office of Public Service the Central Information Technology Unit (CITU) have responsibility for ensuring that the government's response to the problem of the year 2000 date change in its systems is co-ordinated and coherent, that adequate support and advice is given to departments and that progress is monitored.

2.3 The Central Information Technology Unit have commissioned a programme of work from the Central Computer and Telecommunications Agency (CCTA) to raise awareness of the problem, advise departments on best practice, tackle issues of common concern and monitor progress.

2.4 CITU and CCTA are collaborating with the Department of Trade and Industry (DTI) and Taskforce 2000 which involves the private sector in raising awareness of the year 2000 problem in industry and commerce.

2.5 Figure 1 illustrates the relationship between departments and agencies who have responsibility for resolving the problem of the year 2000 date change in the public sector. A brief description of the role of CITU, CCTA and Taskforce 2000 is at Annex 1.

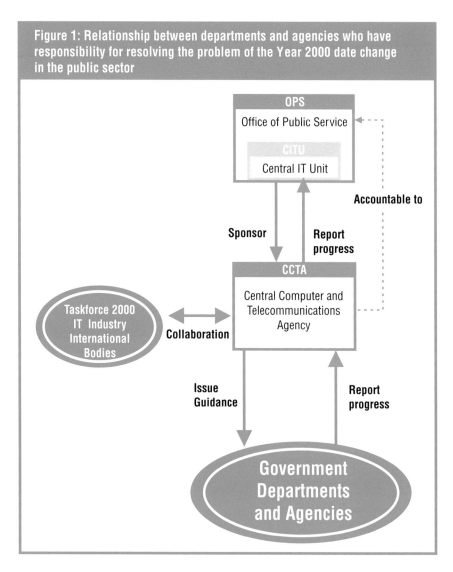

Figure 1: Relationship between departments and agencies who have responsibility for resolving the problem of the Year 2000 date change in the public sector

Programme of action

2.6 CITU supported by CCTA have identified a programme of action to ensure that government's response to the year 2000 problem is co-ordinated and coherent. The programme and the action taken and planned by CCTA and CITU is shown in Box 2.

2.7 The success criteria of this programme are:

✔ all departments should complete an audit of their information systems for year 2000 compliance by January 1997;

✔ all departments should finalise a prioritised, costed, timed programme of action by October 1997;

✔ all departments should have tested all modified systems by January 1999.

Box 2: CCTA/CITU Programme of Action

Fostering work by vendors to tackle the problem

- Guidance issued on legal issues and model clauses for contracts.
- Requirement established that all products in the government IT catalogue are Year 2000 compliant.
- Questionnaire to suppliers regarding compliance of the products. Results to be made known to public sector organisations.

Co-ordinating activity

- Year 2000 Public Sector Group established August 1996 representing central departments and health, police and local government sectors to exchange information, co-ordinate and monitor activity across government. Membership of the group is shown in Annex 2.
- Liaison established with DTI and other groups outside the public sector. A list of groups in regular contact with CCTA is at Annex 3.

Monitoring developments in industry and overseas

- Collaboration with Taskforce 2000 and CSSA.
- Exchange of information with other governments, particularly with the USA, and tracking of advice from industry experts.

CCTA/CITU

Raising awareness

- Leaflets outlining the problem and a checklist of steps to take were produced - April 1996.
- Seminar held for senior civil servants - March 1996.
- Conference held to raise awareness of the problem - April 1996.
- Conferences held on how to get started - September 1996.
- Articles produced for relevant journals and presentations given at public sector events.
- Further articles and presentations will be produced.
- Conference planned for June 1997.

Sharing experience

- Website established on the Internet to provide background material and links to other sources of information - June 1996.
- Internet discussion group set up and run by CCTA to provide a forum for exchange of information and experience - June 1996.
- Guidance volumes to be published May/June 1997.
- A series of booklets are planned for subsequent publication on issues of common concern.

2.8 CITU and CCTA will be reviewing this programme in the light of the results of a survey of departments carried out in January 1997 to see if there are any aspects of guidance and advice which may need a change of emphasis.

Progress

2.9 Although responsibility for maintaining progress rests with individual departments, CCTA conducted a survey of the main departments and smaller organisations in the public sector in December 1996/January 1997. A total of 124 questionnaires were

7

sent out to central departments and their agencies and
79 organisations replied. Of those who did not reply, three were at
departmental level, the remainder were small agencies.

2.10   PA Consulting Group with Taskforce 2000 carried out a survey in
November 1996. This was sent to 535 IT and Business Directors in
public and private sector organisations. 18 per cent of respondents
were from government departments or agencies. The key
conclusions were:

- senior management awareness is increasing but there is still
insufficient understanding of the problem;

- only two thirds of organisations have started an audit and very
few have completed one;

- the majority of organisations do not have a budget for their
audits;

- the anticipated costs of achieving compliance have increased
dramatically but are probably still understated;

- most organisations now believe that they will be affected before
year 2000;

- most organisations think they can fix the problem on time, but
this may be unrealistic.

Awareness

2.11   The PA Consulting Group survey showed a high level of awareness
among senior managers in the public and private sectors (Figure 2)
though only 28 per cent of senior managers were considered to be
fully aware of the problem.

Project stage

2.12   CCTA found that most departments and agencies in their sample are
at the stage of auditing their systems. Figure 3 shows how far
government organisations have reached in their project plans.

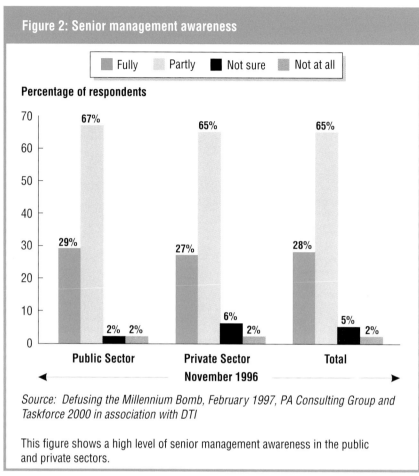

Figure 2: Senior management awareness

This figure shows a high level of senior management awareness in the public and private sectors.

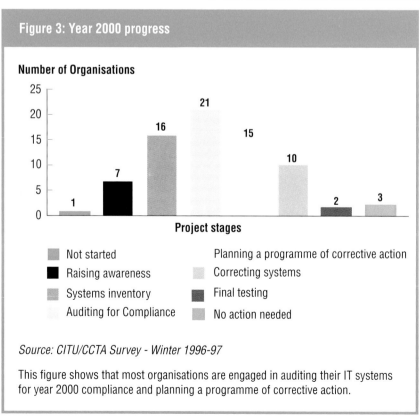

Figure 3: Year 2000 progress

This figure shows that most organisations are engaged in auditing their IT systems for year 2000 compliance and planning a programme of corrective action.

2.13   The private sector has made similar progress. PA Consulting Group found that 72 per cent of private sector organisations in their sample had carried out a full or partial audit compared with 77 per cent in the public sector (Figure 4).

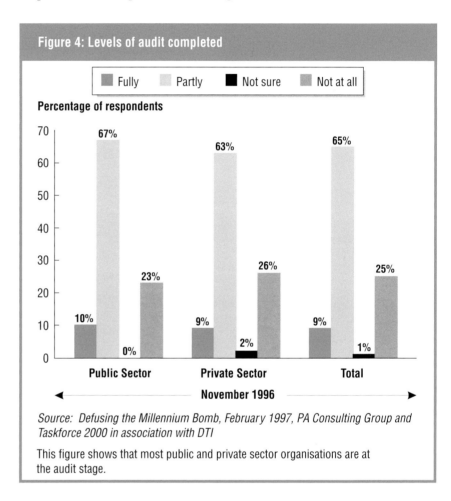

Figure 4: Levels of audit completed

Source: Defusing the Millennium Bomb, February 1997, PA Consulting Group and Taskforce 2000 in association with DTI

This figure shows that most public and private sector organisations are at the audit stage.

Anticipated date of compliance

2.14   80 per cent of government departments and agencies responding to the CCTA survey were confident that they will complete the work in time. Where doubt was expressed about completion, the issues yet to be resolved were mainly about funding, resource availability, testing and compliance of bought in products.

2.15   The organisations responding to the PA Consulting Group survey were a little more optimistic with 95 per cent of public and private organisations in this sample anticipating compliance by the year 2000 (Figure 5). PA Consulting Group, however, cautioned that optimism may be based on inadequate assessment of the risk as, at this stage, very few organisations have fully completed their audits.

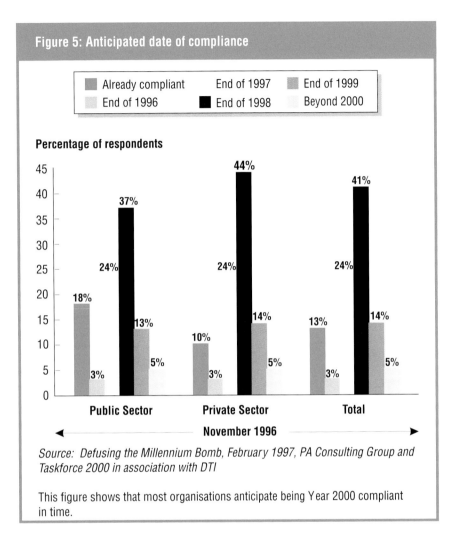

Figure 5: Anticipated date of compliance

Legend: Already compliant | End of 1997 | End of 1999 | End of 1996 | End of 1998 | Beyond 2000

Percentage of respondents

Public Sector: 18%, 3%, 24%, 37%, 13%, 5%
Private Sector: 10%, 3%, 24%, 44%, 14%, 5%
Total: 13%, 3%, 24%, 41%, 14%, 5%

November 1996

Source: *Defusing the Millennium Bomb, February 1997, PA Consulting Group and Taskforce 2000 in association with DTI*

This figure shows that most organisations anticipate being Year 2000 compliant in time.

Costs

2.16 Over half of the organisations responding to the CCTA survey (59 per cent) were unable to provide an estimated cost of their work programme. One fifth of the respondents expected to incur no additional costs. These were all either small agencies where the normal budgeted replacement cycle of IT systems is planned to take place before the year 2000, or organisations that are already year 2000 compliant. A further fifth of the respondents were able to provide estimates which totalled £53 million, most of which was attributable to the Department of Social Security. This figure excludes major departments such as the Ministry of Defence.

2.17 Most departments are still at the stage of auditing their systems and planning a programme of corrective action. Until these stages have been completed it is not possible to estimate the costs across the public sector. Departments have been given a target of October 1997 to complete detailed planning and costing of their programmes. CCTA plan to spend £160,000 in 1996-97 and a similar sum in 1997-98 on year 2000 work.

2.18 Private sector organisations responding to the PA Consulting Group survey are in a similar position with one fifth of them able to estimate costs with some confidence. Focus group interviews conducted as part of this survey confirm that as the problem is better understood, anticipated costs tend to rise. In March 1996 only 4 per cent of organisations surveyed thought it would cost them more than £5 million to solve the problem. In November 1996 19 per cent of organisations estimated it would cost over £5 million including 10 per cent who thought it would cost over £10 million each to solve the problem.

Conclusion

2.19 CITU and CCTA have raised awareness of the problem, issued guidance to help departments and are monitoring progress. Public and private sector organisations have made very similar progress. The responsibility in the public sector for taking action to ensure computers continue to function in the year 2000 lies with individual departments and agencies. The success of the programme will depend on the ability of departments and agencies to manage projects within the timescales set by the Office of Public Service. This is one project where the completion date cannot be slipped. We therefore intend to publish a further report updating progress across departments and agencies.

Annex 1

Roles of key players

Central Information Technology Unit

The Central Information Technology Unit (CITU) is part of the Cabinet Office (Office of Public Service). It has the role of advising Ministers on the development of an IT strategy to enable the Government to improve the efficiency and quality of the services it supplies to businesses and the citizen, as well as improving the efficiency of the Government's internal processes.

Central Computer and Telecommunications Agency

The Central Computer and Telecommunications Agency (CCTA) is an Executive Agency of the Office of Public Service (as of 1 April 1996). Its aim is to improve the delivery of public services by the best use of information technology.

The objective of the Agency is to develop, maintain and make available expertise about information technology, which public sector organisations will draw on in order to operate more effectively and efficiently. In particular it provides: advice and assistance on IT procurement and contracting; advice and assistance in the use of IT; and specific services, in particular in relation to telecommunications.

Taskforce 2000

Taskforce 2000 was formed in 1996 and is a not-for-profit private company with an objective of raising awareness of the year 2000 problem with senior decision makers throughout the UK economy and to mobilise whatever resources are available to achieve this goal. It is funded and supported by DTI and private companies, and includes representatives from the Confederation of British Industry, the Computing Services and Software Association, the Federation of the Electronics Industry and the National Computing Centre.

Annex 2

Membership of Year 2000 Public Sector Group

Central Computer and Telecommunications Agency (Chair)
Central Information Technology Unit
Charity Commission
Companies House
Crown Prosecution Service
Department for Education and Employment
Department of Health
Department of Finance & Personnel (NI)
Department of Social Security
Department of Trade and Industry
Department of the Environment
Export Credits Guarantee Department
Home Office - Police IT Organisation
Home Office - CISU
HM Customs & Excise
HM Land Registry
HM Treasury
Inland Revenue
Isle of Man Government
Local Government Management Board
Ministry of Agriculture, Fisheries and Food
Ministry of Defence
National Audit Office
NHS Executive
Northern Ireland Civil Service
Ordnance Survey
Property Advisors to the Civil Estate (PACE)
Scottish Healthcare Supplies
Society of IT Managers (SOCITM)
Taskforce 2000
The Environment Agency

Annex 3

Organisations in regular contact with CCTA

British Standards Institute (BSI)

Computer Services and Software Association (CSSA)

Department of Trade and Industry

European Union Public Procurement Group (PPG)

Group of 7 Government Online Project (G7 GOL)

IT Service Management Forum (ITSMF)

KPMG Impact Group

Local Government Management Board (LGMB)

Society of IT Managers (SOCITM)

Taskforce 2000

US Government

Various other overseas governments

Bird and Bird Solicitors

De Jager and Associates

various IT suppliers including EDS, Eurocrest, Greenwich Meantime, IBM (UK), ICL, Millennium UK, Parity, Pink Elephant

Reports by the Comptroller and Auditor General Session 1997-98

The Comptroller and Auditor General has to date, in Session 1997-98, presented to the House of Commons the following reports under Section 9 of the National Audit Act, 1983:

Printed in the UK for The Stationery Office Limited on behalf of
the Controller of Her Majesty's Stationery Office
Dd 5066440   5/97   480003   220000   J13562   108393

Published by The Stationery Office Limited
and available from:

The Publications Centre
(Mail, telephone and fax orders only)
PO Box 276, London SW8 5DT
General enquiries 0171 873 0011
Telephone orders 0171 873 9090
Fax orders 0171 873 8200

The Stationery Office Bookshops
49 High Holborn, London WC1V 6HB
(counter service and fax orders only)
Fax 0171 831 1326
68-69 Bull Street, Birmingham B4 6AD
0121 236 9696 Fax 0121 236 9699
33 Wine Street, Bristol BS1 2BQ
0117 9264306 Fax 0117 9294515
9-21 Princess Street, Manchester M60 8AS
0161 834 7201 Fax 0161 833 0634
16 Arthur Street, Belfast BT1 4GD
01232 238451 Fax 01232 235401
The Stationery Office Oriel Bookshop
The Friary, Cardiff CF1 4AA
01222 395548 Fax 01222 384347
71 Lothian Road, Edinburgh EH3 9AZ
(counter service only)

In addition customers in Scotland may mail,
telephone or fax their orders to:
Scottish Publication Sales,
South Gyle Crescent, Edinburgh EH12 9EB
0131 479 3141 Fax 0131 479 3142

The Parliamentary Bookshop
12 Bridge Street, Parliament Square,
London SW1A 2JX
Telephone orders 0171 219 3890
General enquiries 0171 219 3890
Fax orders 0171 219 3866

Accredited Agents
(see Yellow Pages)

and through good booksellers

£4.70

ISBN 0-10-260698-6

Government response
to the Foot and Mouth Disease
2007 Review

Presented to Parliament by the Secretary of State for Environment, Food and Rural Affairs
by Command of Her Majesty
February 2009

Cm 7514

£14.35

OX	R

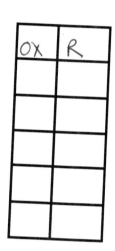

Government response
to the Foot and Mouth Disease
2007 Review

Presented to Parliament by the Secretary of State for Environment, Food and Rural Affairs
by Command of Her Majesty
February 2009

Cm 7514

£14.35

© **Crown Copyright 2009**

The text in this document (excluding the Royal Arms and other departmental or agency logos) may be reproduced free of charge in any format or medium providing it is reproduced accurately and not used in a misleading context. The material must be acknowledged as Crown copyright and the title of the document specified.

Where we have identified any third party copyright material you will need to obtain permission from the copyright holders concerned.

For any other use of this material please write to Office of Public Sector Information, Information Policy Team, Kew, Richmond, Surrey TW9 4DU or e-mail: licensing@opsi.gov.uk

ISBN: 978 010 175142 1